Sam's ba

Story by Annette Smith
Illustrations by Pat Reynolds

Here comes a clown.

Look at the balloons.

Sam said,

"Mom!

Look at the balloons."

Sam said,

"Mom!

Look at the balloons.

Come on!"

"**No balloons?**" said Sam.

"Here is a balloon,"

said the clown.

"Look at the clown,"

said Mom.

"Look at the **balloon**!"

said Sam.

"My balloon is a dog,"

said Sam.